# How to Hire the Ones You Won't Want to Fire

*The Art of Pulling Back Their Mask to Really Know
the Person You're About to Hire*

*By*

## *Ryan Englin and Jeremy Macliver*

Find us online and learn more at:
HireBetterPeopleFaster.com

# CONTENTS

Setting proper expectations on both sides is critical to success.

Using the interview process as your competitive advantage.

Taking the next right step will change the way your company grows.

# Prologue

.........................

My name is Ryan Englin – Core Fit Hiring™ Coach – and I'm Jeremy Macliver – Certified EOS Implementer®. Many business leaders tell us their number one issue is people. People issues are a leading reason why companies seek out an EOS Implementer®, and it's also why they hire a Core Fit Hiring Coach.

We wrote this book for these frustrated business leaders. Whether it's retention, engagement, or productivity, the Core Fit Hiring System will help you address and solve the problem. Specifically, we'll dive into how you can unmask a candidate and reveal their true work identity – *before* you hire them.

How do you quickly discover who people *really* are? What do these screenings and interviews look like? Implementing our steps can take your business to the next level. When you hire right, many of your people issues will go away. It's just one piece of the overall Core Fit Hiring System, and we're breaking it down for you here.

This book comes from real world experience. We've both been in the trenches like you. The two of us will be sharing some personal stories on how we came to develop this process. We'll walk you through what we did wrong and all that we learned. And then we'll show you the process we built to make sure it never happens again.

Before reading any further, visit our website at HireBetterPeopleFaster.com to register for the tools we share and to access additional training about the Core Fit Hiring System.

# SECTION 1

# Can You Relate?

......................................

**Why So Many Interviews Fail to Show You the Real Person.**

*I*t was my very first hire. I was 19, and I remember the interview like it was yesterday.

> In the hour we spent together, we laughed, talked, and asked each other questions about the position.
>
> He wanted a company where he could grow professionally.
>
> He had the skills to do the job.
>
> And, he said everything I wanted to hear.
>
> The interview went fast. It was easy. It was evident to me he was the right fit for the job.
>
> A week passed between the interview and his start date, and I could not wait for him to begin. Day one was training, and he shadowed me on the job. He followed along and was pleasant, and everything went

*as planned. Then, for some reason, a sinking feeling deep down began to creep in. Something wasn't right.*

*Four weeks later, after I had let him go, a manager I originally had sit in on the interview said, "That one surprised me. He was completely different on the job than in the interview."*

*Was he a fraud? Or was there something wrong with our process? Was it a combination of the two? In this book, we'll address how to reduce the chances of the first issue (fraud) and refine the second (process).*

*Over the years, I've hired hundreds of people. Some were amazing. As for others, well, I wanted to fire the person who hired them.*

\* \* \*

Everything we are sharing in this book came from being in the hiring trenches and watching what worked and what did not. Each step has been tested and challenged.

We have used it in building several companies of our own, and now we coach companies in various industries to implement the Core Fit Hiring System.

We will walk you through our interview process and explain what is going on at each stage. We'll also provide tips on how to stay in control, because peeling back a person's layers can be difficult. But with our help, you'll soon understand that unmasking them and getting to know who they really are upfront is vital. And it's possible.

We developed this process to increase the odds the person we are interviewing is going to be the person we hire. Often, we find ourselves falling in love with an applicant too soon and overlooking a glaring sign, failing to uncover some misaligned traits. A process can help us stay focused and objective while we interview.

When our clients follow this process, they build the skills to filter out the impostors early on. Furthermore, following this process makes it easier to fire people when the process breaks down. When you design a well-oiled, effective system, you can locate issues promptly.

Before diving in, we want to be clear that we're making a few assumptions about you.

1. Your job description clearly outlines what it's like to work at your company.
2. Your job description clearly outlines what you expect of the applicant.
3. Your communication with the applicant during the process is quick and timely.
4. You know precisely whom the right person is for joining your team.
5. You can clearly articulate what success looks like for the employee using terms they can understand.

This book is focusing on the interview process. If you would like to learn more about how to improve any of the above points, go to HireBetterPeopleFaster.com and check out our resources.

We're going to review the four steps to this interview process.

- Résumé and Application Review
- Pre-Screen Interview (often a phone interview)
- In-Person Interview(s)
- The Pullback Offer

These steps build on each other, to create a recruiting funnel – where each step eliminates a significant amount of the applicant pool. Our focus is always on hiring the right person for both your company culture and the position. The Core Fit Hiring Process we're outlining here will help you do just that.

# SECTION 2

# Résumé and Application Review

.................................

*There are two types of résumés in existence today: those written by professional résumé writers and those written by people who don't know how to write résumés. Both are garbage during the screening process.*

**— Ryan Englin**

**Applications Can Tell You So Much About Applicants if You Know What to Look For**

It's vital you don't judge an applicant's résumé too harshly. Most people don't know how to write a good résumé. Furthermore, past performance is ***not*** an indicator of future success.

Just because someone has had success in the past doesn't guarantee it will happen in the future at your company. The inverse is also true. Because so many things impact someone's ability to perform, use the résumé as a screening tool, but not as a hiring tool.

This is the first step in unmasking the applicant - getting to know the real person you are interviewing. If you know what to look for in this first stage, you're setting yourself up for the right hire weeks from now.

So, what should you be looking for in a résumé or application?

---

CORE FIT HIRING TIP: There are some job seekers who won't have a résumé. Historically, their industry hasn't asked for them. You'll know if the position you're posting falls into this category. If so, do not require a résumé as part of the application process. It will severely limit your applicant pool. You can still request it, just don't require it.

---

**Patterns in Their Work History**

First and foremost, look for patterns.

- Do they have a history of job-hopping?

- What is their average stay at the job? Is it comparable to the industry standards? Is it acceptable in your organization?

- Do they seem to land jobs in the same position, or are they continually switching the type of work they do?

- Do they stay in one industry? If they bounce from one industry to another, are they doing similar work?

- Do they have any significant gaps in their work history? Remember, it's unlikely they stopped working. They may just not want to share.

- Do they provide an amount of detail in the résumé similar to the amount of detail necessary for this new position?

As you look for patterns in the résumé or application, consider your expectations about the roles they will be filling. It is important that they meet the patterns you think acceptable. If they are showing a history of bad patterns, there isn't any reason to move forward.

## Consider the Role You're Filling

As you look over their résumé and application, make sure you consider the work they'll be doing. We've found that great technicians don't always type in complete sentences. They can have a bunch of punctuation mistakes and format their résumé in the most non-design-friendly way. When screening their résumé, we don't worry too much about this. We aren't expecting them to be spelling and grammar experts to deliver our service. Ultimately, we are looking to see if their answers show us any signs that they won't work out well on our team. On the other hand, if they will be building reports or communicating with clients, it's best to evaluate the way they write. If you are not impressed with their quality of written communication now, you probably won't be after you've hired them. We encourage you also to be wary of the perfect résumé. It's likely much of it is embellished for your reading pleasure. Indeed, it's likely that it's a mask, the very thing we want to remove.

Look for patterns that point toward the things you can't teach like work ethic, attention to detail, consistency in communication, and their desire to stay focused on a career path. The primary purpose of reviewing applications and résumés is to confirm they have the necessary skills and to look for any patterns you don't want in your company.

We need these clues to effectively uncover their true self. A little systematic digging around in this first stage leads to thorough excavation in the long run.

# SECTION 3

# The Pre-Screen Interview

..........................

*Most people can't find good help because they haven't defined good help*

— Jeremy Macliver

**Gain and Maintain Control of the Pre-Screen Interview, and Uncover the Real Person on the Other Side**

Now it's time to move forward with a couple of outstanding applicants. You've successfully peeled back layers by reviewing applications and résumés. Now, you need a simple way to discover who they really are. So, how do you eliminate the wrong people and avoid spending precious time on them?

Depending on the volume of applicants, there are two ways to handle this step in the process.

1. You call them to have a short conversation.
2. You have them call you for the same short conversation, giving them a list of pre-determined times to do so.

Regardless of who calls whom, the first 10 seconds of the call set the pace, and it's during these crucial seconds most hiring managers lose control.

This is not time to get chatty. The entire point is to reveal the applicant's true character. How can you do that if you're hogging the spotlight?

In this all too familiar example, one client continued making hires that weren't turning out to be good employees. After listening to a couple of the interview calls, we found they were making the dreaded mistake of talking way too much way too early in the call.

For almost fifteen minutes, the business owner spoke about the company, the vision, and long-term goals. Throughout the call, the applicant shared their excitement about the direction and being on the team. Everything went well. The owner decided to fast-track them through the interview process. Less than six weeks later, the owner was letting them go.

In all of the rapport building, the owner gave the applicant everything they needed to restate the perfect answers. The owner helped the applicant put pieces of their mask back on. That's not what we're after. We want to break down walls and get to know someone for whom they truly are.

Not surprisingly, more and more job seekers are adept at knowing what to say to ace the interview. They research. They rehearse. They act. They design suitable, coverall responses to your typical interview questions.

This has to change. It's time to make them uncomfortable. It's time to disrupt them.

**CORE FIT HIRING TIP**: Remember, the pre-screen interview is about the applicant. The pre-screen interview is NOT ABOUT YOU. They're already sold on your company, so you shouldn't be talking about you, and you definitely should not be "building rapport." There's plenty of time to get to know them later.

## Purpose of the Pre-Screen Interview

There is only one purpose of the pre-screen interview – to make sure they're worth your time in interviewing them further.

If they aren't going to be a fit in your organization, it's better to know upfront. We recommend you spend the first 90% of the interview **convinced they will not fit**. Interviewing in this way can be extremely hard when you need to fill many positions. But even when the need is high, we encourage you to take this mindset. Ignoring this will cause turnover to continue chipping away at your profits.

## First, Push Them Away

When starting the phone interview, keep the small talk to a minimum. Truly learning about someone isn't supposed to feel super cozy.

Make sure they have the time to talk, uninterrupted. Then jump right into the questions that will help you screen the applicant at this stage. It may feel a bit abrupt and impersonal. Just remember, there's plenty of time to be friends after you hire them. Right now, it's about finding the right fit for your team.

> *I remember one leader stepping out with a little blind faith in this process. He said for the first part of the interview, he was doing his best to push the applicant away, but it didn't feel natural. Then the applicant said something that startled the leader.*
>
> *Because the leader was actively pushing them away, he wasn't emotionally connected. He was able to recognize what he didn't want and explore it further.*

> *He later told us that "all of a sudden, I wanted to push them away." Ultimately, he didn't hire them and was grateful for it. Hiring this individual would have hurt the company's future.*

The pre-screen interview should be the same for all applicants. You should ask the same four or five questions, in the same order. Do not share with the applicant whether it was a good answer. However, it's okay to repeat their answer back to make sure you understand it correctly.

Remember, you can be friends later. This process should take no more than fifteen minutes. This is perhaps your first live conversation. Realize that you're talking to a tightly buttoned-up version of the applicant. The goal here is to decide if you want to invite them in for a longer interview.

All the while, you're hunting for alignment with your company's culture and core values. Keep that as your focus. Some questions to ask at this stage might be:

- Why do you want to work for our company?
- What about our company's mission compelled you to apply?
- How would you define success?
- What does <insert your core value> mean to you?

You may notice none of these questions have to do with the position, or the applicant's skill set. They're about what's truly important to you and your company. Asking people to share their definition of a term can be incredibly eye-opening. When their definition is too vague or too far away from yours, it's a good sign they won't be a good fit.

You're getting to know the person and their real motivations. It's hard to fake a solid answer to the wide-open question "What does *excellence* mean to you?" If you're listening when they respond, you'll hear how this person thinks and behaves.

If your company hasn't yet defined your core values, visit our website at HireBetterPeopleFaster.com for some assistance.

**Then Pull Them In**

The best thing about starting the interview process with a pre-screen phone call is it is easier to adjust the time of the meeting.

If, early on, you decide this person isn't going to be a fit, just conclude the meeting. You've met the person behind the mask, and they're just not promising for your company.

Regardless of your decision to move forward with them, concluding the call is the same.

Concluding the meeting means that you move into pulling them in, even if you're not hiring them. You've spent the entire call "convinced" they aren't the right fit, and you've pushed them away. Now it's time to switch and pull the applicant in.

Sell them on why your company is excellent. You want to end the interview with them excited and hopeful that they get to work for you, even if you don't want them right now. The truth is, the more fans you can have outside your company, the better options you will have in the future.

If you don't want to hire them, let them know you are doing more interviews, and you will keep them posted if they move to the next phase. If you want to move to the next step, schedule the meeting right then – no reason to make them wait.

We'll say it again, you can't have too many fans out there. And we actually have a process for keeping the applicants you didn't hire informed about the company. Still, for this book, we are just going to focus on the interviewing and selection process.

# SECTION 4

# The In-Person Interview

*Find someone that fits your team's values, and they'll
learn whatever skills they need.*

**— Ryan Englin**

.........................

**How to Find the Right Fit for Your Company and
the Position**

The in-person interview is your opportunity to
confirm the candidate is the right fit for both the
company and the position. Their application and pre-
screen have impressed you so far. But you're still out
to discover the real person you are interviewing.

How do you keep the unmasking momentum going?
How do you access the true character of the person
who might someday soon be working for you?

Just like the phone interview, you want to make sure they are present and ready to go. Don't rehash the last conversation. Now is not the time to be friends. You want to go right back into the "I'm not convinced you are the right person" mindset.

## Again, Push Them Away

You'll spend most of the interview pushing them away. Don't come across as a jerk (unless you naturally are one). Remember, authenticity is key. After all, authenticity is what we want. If you come across as authentic and trustworthy, they may do the same. Conversely, if you're not authentic, likely, they won't be either. You want to see the real person you are interviewing, so let them see the real person and company interviewing them.

At this stage, you need to be more interested in how they process the answer than the actual answer. Let them do most of the talking. Dan Sullivan, the founder of Strategic Coach, talks about always being the buyer. Remember, you are the buyer, and it is their job to sell you. As leaders, we often sell people on our ideas. Now is not the time for that.

You, as the interviewer, are the buyer. You need to remain in that position until you have the person you're looking for, and you're ready to move forward.

Be a smart buyer. Don't fall for the gimmicks and feel-good deals. Often, it's easy to reach for a "great buy" if it's there in front of you. And especially if you're desperate. Don't trust emotions and hype. Be objective. Assess how they process questions and ideas. Then later, you won't be stuck with a great deal that turned out to be a bust.

## ARE THEY RIGHT FOR OUR COMPANY?

We recommend that you focus on future behavioral interview questions in the first half of the interview.

For more on picking the right questions, go to HireBetterPeopleFaster.com

Watch and listen to how they process their answers. If at any time during the interview you become convinced they are not the right person, move to conclude and wrap up the meeting. Not everyone is going to be a good hire, and that's okay. Don't waste your time getting them to fit. You'll only regret it later.

**ARE THEY RIGHT FOR THE JOB?**

Once you've completed the culture fit, move into a skills assessment. There are many ways to test their skills.

Remember human beings make mistakes, and if they want the job, they may be nervous. Allow them to make some mistakes. Mistakes are part of being real. In fact, when people make mistakes, masks usually come down. You'll see discomfort. Mistakes disrupt the flow. They're good things because you get to see the candidate's reaction to problems, misunderstandings, and confusion.

Finally, put more weight into how they solve a problem than whether or not they solve it your way – there's plenty of time to teach them your process later.

> *When I owned the body shops, we would give the applicant an estimate we were working on to test their skills. We would ask them to see what else they could find. We would leave them alone for about 10 minutes with the car.*
>
> *They would come back with additions to the estimate, particularly what they thought we would want to see. But we were more interested in how they processed it than in what they wrote. We knew they couldn't get a perfect estimate in only a few minutes, but we could see them work.*
>
> *Often, we would put something on the estimate that wasn't needed. Some would call us out on it. When this happened, we knew we had a strong candidate that was going to take care of our relationships with*

*the insurance companies. Others would fluff the estimate with things that weren't necessary just to impress us in the interview. It revealed their character. In this ten-minute part of the interview process, we got a glimpse into their character, how detailed they were, how knowledgable they really were, and how they would take care of our insurance partners. It is important to watch these behaviors as objectively as possible. It reveals how they will work for you in the future.*

You will want to put candidates in a setting similar to what they will be in once they have the job.

**Here are some ideas:**

- If you are hiring for a sales position
    - ○ Have them do some role playing during the interview.
    - ○ For phone sales, put them in another room and have them call you.
    - ○ If they have to talk to engineering, give them a request from a customer and see

how they deliver it to your engineering team.

- If computer skills are required
  - o Have them do one of the many online tests for Office, Excel, or QuickBooks.
  - o Have them take a call and capture notes at the same time.
- If they are a craft worker
  - o Have them perform the skill, e.g. do a weld for you.
  - o Give them a problem to solve and have them show you how they solve it.
- If they have to diagnose issues, e.g. in a service technician role
  - o Roleplay a customer conversation.
  - o Give them the problem and ask them to diagnose through Q&A.

o Give them a simple set of problems or more complex ones, and see how they troubleshoot.

These are just a few of the examples we've used in the past. Use these ideas to develop your own version of the in-person interview.

Once again, the right answers are not as important as how they process the answer. Perfect answers have been researched and rehearsed. What is most important is to disrupt them and notice the approach the candidate takes. Their process is part of their real identity. It's what will matter greatly to your company's success.

## Concluding the In-Person Interview

Once you are clear on their skills, conclude the meeting. Just like the phone interview, it is time to switch from pushing to pulling. Now share all the great things about working in your company and your vision for it.

Get excited, and let them get excited with you. Create the raving fan, even if you aren't going to hire them. And if you know they're the one, start the next stage of the process immediately. There's no reason to let them leave so they can keep looking for another job.

# SECTION 5

# The Introduction Test

*When you're interviewing someone, their goal is to get hired. When you introduce them to your team, the goal is to make a friend. Sometimes you'll see a totally different person that you may have missed.*

**— Jeremy Macliver**

........................

**Including you Team in the Process Can Multiply Your Results**

If the applicant processes key issues in a way aligned to how you operate, what you value, and the skills you require, it is time to do one more screen before you make them an offer.

After concluding the in-person interview, invite the applicant to meet some of the team members. We coach our clients to teach a handful of the co-workers how to interview. The employees know they are a part of the interview process. We've had some "fantastic" applicants fail the interview process at this stage.

The introduction test is a formal application of letting candidates be themselves. The mask usually falls away here more than it does at any other stage. The cultivated, robot version shuts down. True colors are revealed.

As soon as candidates meet their peers, their guard goes down. They're confident you will offer them the job. There's no reason for them to continue to put on a show. After a quick introduction, make sure you're conveniently pulled away to something else. Leaving them alone with a future co-worker, they may share things or act in a way counter to what you've already seen.

*I remember one guy; I took him out in the shop. I introduced him to a future co-worker, and then went over to take care of something else. When I had been present with the applicant and the co-worker, everyone was engaged in the conversation. After walking away, the applicant became distant and put out. He would give short, vague answers, acting as if he was above his peers. He dodged questions and moved around as if he had better things to do.*

*I didn't catch it, because when I came back, he was incredibly engaging with me. I then took him to a couple of other co-workers.*

*I thanked him for his time and told him we would follow up in a couple of days. I was still positive he was the right guy. As was my custom, I asked the three co-workers what they thought. I was shocked when the first one reported back how he acted when I wasn't there. To my surprise, he had treated all three in a similar manner. All three gave him a thumbs down on hiring. I couldn't believe it and begrudgingly decided to pass on him.*

It is important to trust the feedback you receive from the introduction test. Your employees are often able to see their future co-worker in a way you cannot. As a bonus, when you've selected the correct person, these co-workers will know you've included them in on the decision. They will work to make sure this new hire is successful.

# The Pullback Offer

*If you're losing people in the first 90 days of employment,*
*it's because expectations weren't set or weren't met.*

— **Ryan Englin**

........................

## Setting Proper Expectations on Both Sides Is Critical to Success

Okay. The stars have aligned. The candidate has been vetted in your process, and they still make sense for your company. They are a match in core values, skills, work ethic, peer relations, etc. The person sitting in front of you is the one. It's destiny that they are here. You're now ready to give them the job.

**STOP!**

Before you do, it's time to pull back. Hard. The Pullback Offer™ takes everything you've learned about the person and puts it through one final check point.

Why?

It's your last chance at unmasking them. It's your last chance to disrupt them.

The interview is like dating someone new, and the offer is equivalent to a proposal for marriage.

We don't date someone for just an hour or two and then ask them to marry us, do we?

So, why would we do the same when hiring someone without having a conversation about expectations? And what happens when one of us lets the other down?

That's where the Pullback Offer comes in.

It's ridiculous to think we'll interview someone for days, weeks, or even months before hiring them. Which is exactly why we need a process to fast-track what we learn about someone.

Here's how it works.

1. Let them know you're ready to make them an offer.

2. Tell them that before you ask them to make a decision about moving forward with the job, you need to have a real, open, honest conversation about working together. And, if you have any sense that they're going to decline an offer, make sure to address it before moving forward. There's no reason to spend time on this process if we know up front it's not going to work out.

3. Address any issues/concerns that came up during the interview process.

4. Address any issues that didn't come up during the interview but should have.

5. Address any issues you think they will have working at your company. Share challenges they may face in dealing with certain company processes, managers, or work environment.

6. Conclude the meeting with an accepted or declined offer.

Regardless of the outcome, you win. If either of you decides to decline/rescind the offer, it's okay. They aren't the right person. Remember, we're on a mission to unmask and disrupt – all so we can select authentic employees. You must make sure you're hiring someone who aligns with your company's goals and will be a valuable member of your team.

It is important to share any issues your organization may create for the new employee.

*A while back, I had a client that was a high-quality, expert micro-manager, and he knew it.*

*The business was the owner's baby. He built it from the ground up, and he was very particular about how people performed the work, dealt with the clients, and managed internal processes. No one was going to do it differently than he would, and he made it very clear by being involved in every single process.*

*While this is incredibly inefficient, there was no changing it. He was confident in the way he ran his company. So, we addressed his behavior during the Pullback Offer with every single candidate. He would explain to the candidate that this was the way things were. If you had new ideas and you liked to create new processes without his direction, you wouldn't last long.*

## People Don't Leave Jobs; They Leave Managers

The Pullback Offer is the perfect time to let them know who they'll be working for and avoid surprises on either side. As you're learning about their authentic self, don't pretend you are something you're not. It's counterproductive.

When done correctly, the Pullback Offer will set the stage for a successful onboard. There will be fewer surprises from everyone, and working through issues will be second nature.

Here's the general rule on what to talk about during this stage: **If you think it, say it**. Give the candidate permission for this as well. It'll change the quality of people you hire forever.

It's not enough to hire them and deal with it later. If you're going to have an issue, deal with it upfront, before it becomes an issue.

Unmask, disrupt, and select the right fit. This isn't a feel-good game we should be playing. Not even as we make the offer. If we play to bend someone's nature and deep motivations to fit us, that's going to backfire nearly every time. You'll keep hiring people you *think* are right instead of people you *know* are right.

You'll find that when you have these types of open conversations during the interview process, your employees will be more engaged. And engagement leads to them helping you solve problems faster. Turnover decreases. Profit increases, and it becomes a lot more fun to lead. Engaged employees don't leave you over $0.25 more an hour. They'll be a team player for the long haul.

The clarity that you will gain and the trust you will build by having these authentic, honest conversations will exponentially improve your hiring success.

# SECTION 7

# Advanced Interview Techniques

*The best way to stand out as an employer is to offer them*
*a hiring experience unlike anything they've seen before.*

## — Ryan Englin

....................................

## Using the Interview Process as Your Competitive Advantage

The interview can be one of your company's competitive advantages. While your competition is hiring everyone that shows up, you're making the strategic decision to pass on anyone who doesn't fit within your company.

You've established a process that allows you to disrupt and see through interview facades.

Patrick Lencioni, author of The Five Dysfunctions of a Team, says, "If you could get all of the people in an organization rowing the same direction, you could dominate any industry, in any market, at any time." You've made the commitment to build that team and screen only for the best.

One of the best ways to interview is by keeping the interview consistent and objective.

Through the years, we've developed some tools that help build this process. They'll cut down on time spent with the applicant and increase your ability to be objective about them.

While this list isn't exhaustive, it addresses the techniques we find are most likely to be adopted by the team. There's no reason to use any of them unless one speaks to you. By no means should you work to incorporate all of them. They'll work best when you find you're no longer getting the results you want and need something different to break through.

## Answer Rating

Before moving to the next question in the interview process, we've found that taking the time to score the applicant's response to the current question on a scale of 1-5 allows for a consistent review of the applicants' answers.

Don't overthink it. Just put the number down that you feel at that moment. It will be surprisingly accurate. We've interviewed with multiple interviewers in the room, and it can be astonishing how we will all rate certain questions the same. If you and the other interviewer rate the response drastically different, it allows you to have a productive conversation after the interview and determine why you each viewed the answer so differently.

Instead of taking notes, listen to their response. Often, we find that when we listen to their answer and how they respond, it's easier to enter a number. At the end of the interview, you can add up the points. After interviewing several people over several days, scoring applicants becomes a great way to compare notes.

> **CORE FIT HIRING TIP**: Decide beforehand what a 1, 3, and 5 answer sounds like. Give the answer key to the interviewers so it removes subjectivity.

## Multiple Interviewers

Using multiple interviewers during the same interview can be extremely effective, especially if you're the type that loves every candidate. Most often, two people won't fall in love with the same candidate. Both are seeing the person from a different perspective. It also allows both interviewers to alternate between observing and questioning. When one is asking a question, the other person can watch the response.

One challenge that comes up is time management. When you are interviewing on your own, and you recognize the applicant is not a good fit, it is easy to move to conclude. This gets harder when you have multiple interviewers in the room. We recommend that you create a non-verbal way to communicate. We've seen interviewing teams agree that moving their pen from the left to the right side of their notes means "I'm done."

Whatever you and your co-interviewer(s) decide, make sure you have an agreement on how you can move the interview forward without discussing it. In the same manner, teams have created other non-verbal ways of communicating when they wanted to offer someone a job. If interviewer A gets up and gets another pen (this being their previously agreed upon cue), then it is up to interviewer B, as long as they agree, to initiate the conversation about the job offer. This allows both interviewers to communicate, but not jump into something that the other one isn't convinced of yet.

On the other hand, if your company has open and honest conversations, have the conversation right there in front of the candidate. Ask them for a minute for you to discuss whether or not to offer them the position right in front of them. You'll be amazed at what this does. You'll show them you walk the talk.

## Offsite Interviews

If you have someone who needs to be professional in different environments, sometimes a lunch interview or errand interview can make sense. It is a lot more natural for the person, and you can see how they show up in those environments. Just make sure you have an agenda to keep this consistent between candidates.

Let's say they'll be working with a lot of vendors. You could bring them along to pick up some supplies.

Have a couple of "get to know you" questions ready to go for the car ride. When you get to the vendor's office, introduce them and watch the interaction. If you want to plan ahead, let the vendor know you're bringing a candidate with you and ask them to show them around and provide you feedback afterwards.

## Group Interviews

Group interviews with multiple candidates at the same time can be a lot of fun. They can also be a lot of work. Having 6-10 people in the room, all applying for the same position can create some interesting dynamics. We recommend you have a couple of interviewers if you are going to do group interviews. Here are a couple ways to handle group interviews.

You can choose to do a round table, or you can do a conversational style. The roundtable is a little easier on notetaking and keeping track. We recommend starting with one person and going around the room with the same question. After everyone has answered, double-check that no one has anything else to add to their response. Then start with a new person in the group for the next question. You may discover that the person who is strong and engaging when it is their turn becomes completely unplugged and disinterested when it isn't. You will find people who are willing to dismiss other candidates. Some will interject out of turn. Watch for the behaviors you value and the ones that you don't want on the team.

The conversational style interview is where you put the question out to the group and let them answer. This can get a bit messy, but you are not focusing on the answers. You're looking for who emerges as a leader. Some will be strong. Some will want to take center stage, but they won't disagree. Some won't talk. Surprisingly, we've seen some put others down right there in front of everyone. Either way, group interviews offer some great opportunity to see how people will react in competitive situations and in situations where they must work with others.

**Reference Checking**

Reference checking can be tough. Most people are going to put their best references on the application, which makes this process somewhat difficult to keep consistent.

One of the best techniques we've seen for checking references is to ask the candidate to schedule the reference checks for you. They are responsible for contacting their old boss at the companies *you select* from their résumé.

It works like this.

1. You select 3-5 of their old positions from their résumé. If they don't have a résumé, you ask them about their work history.

2. It's on the candidate to reach out to their old boss and set up the reference check call.

3. You speak with their old boss.

**A couple of things to note here:**

When doing reference checks, confirm with your legal team what questions you are allowed to ask and which ones you're not. Some questions can get you into trouble.

Always confirm the legitimacy of their reference to make sure it's their ex-boss you're actually speaking with.

If they don't have the work history or can't get in touch with an old employer, think of other people you'd be comfortable speaking to. This could be a school instructor, leaders where they volunteer, or even classmates they've worked on a project with.

One thing to remember: past performance is NOT an indicator of future success. So, make this about their past behaviors and less about the work they did.

**Personality Profiling**

Behavioral assessments are a great way to identify the person's real behaviors before you offer them the job. There are two assessments we prefer. When profiling someone, it's best to know both WHY and HOW they work. This insight will support you with both onboarding and engaging your new hire.

- ProScan assessments look at why they behave the way they do. We prefer ProScan because it allows the person to complete the assessment and identify stressors in their life. These stressors may be causing them to burn energy dealing with things that could eventually lead to burnout.

- Kolbe A assessments look at how someone will behave. It helps to identify how people naturally process their work. If the job requires them to process data, follow a process, think outside the box, or something extremely technical, you want it to be within their natural behaviors.

Using both of these tools together will help you assess the type of person you're going to get for your team. Check with your HR compliance team as there are EEOC (Equal Employment Opportunity Commission) requirements in using these assessments as part of the hiring process. Because of the investments associated with them, we recommend using them later in the process. Using them later will give you a better picture of whom you ultimately decide to hire.

**Integrity Testing**

Integrity tests will allow you to identify those individuals who have a disposition toward lying, theft, violence, or drug and alcohol use on the job. These assessments are only EEOC-compliant when used pre-hire and must follow specific rules to remain compliant. Some have a 94% or higher accuracy rate and can make a long-term difference in the performance of your team.

Many organizations that implement integrity assessments also find it improves their EMR, or the Experience Modification Rate, for workers compensation insurance, due to fewer false work comp claims.

For more information about personality assessments or integrity testing, visit our website at HireBetterPeopleFaster.com.

Each of these techniques and even combinations of them can help you carve away the fluff and really get to know candidates. These methods often put candidates on their toes and potentially outside their comfort zones.

Most of all, these additions to your interviewing process can assist you in removing any disguises that are keeping you from making the most informed decisions about who you hire.

# SECTION 8

# Getting Started

*The best time to plant a tree was 20 years ago. The second- best time is now.*

**— Chinese Proverb**

............................

**Taking the Next Right Step Will Change the Way Your Company Grows**

We know there's a lot here. There's also a lot we didn't cover.

When developing or changing your interview process, it's imperative you consult with your HR compliance person or legal team. They will make sure you aren't violating any federal, state, or local laws when it comes to interviewing. It's an incredibly nuanced area, and even well-intentioned questions can be the basis for a lawsuit.

That said, an objective interview process can be a game-changer for your business. We've seen clients have candidates who didn't get the job, later refer their friends and family, or even reapply in the future.

If you're struggling to find enough good people for your business, the interview is the lynchpin. It defines when and whom you hire in a way other processes cannot. It's your first line of contact. If you take the time early on to learn who about you are hiring, you will not be overwhelmed with surprises and confusion later.

Make the decision to start hiring for fit and values alignment today. A productive, engaged team member is one of the most valuable assets your company will ever have. It can mean the difference between you winning or losing to your competition.

There are entire HR roles that exist for the sole purpose of developing the interview process. So, don't be discouraged if this feels hard to do, because it is. We're here to help you get this process developed so you can focus on attracting and hiring great employees.

This process will take some time, and it will require you to iterate both the questions and the process. Feel free to experiment with what feels right for your company to get the results you want.

And we're here for you every step of this process. For downloadable tools, to learn more, or contact us directly visit HireBetterPeopleFaster.com.

Get access to all of our published tools and bonus materials for free when you register on our website.

# __Build Your People Process:__

Attract, Hire & Retain the Best

You're results-driven. So are we. Let's take your company to the next level. Join us for a free webinar that shares how to tap into your team's full potential with our complete Core Fit Hiring System.

From determining what you want and who you want, to selecting, onboarding, and developing great employees, the Core Fit Hiring System takes out the mystery and gets to the root of building a great team. Employee engagement isn't a myth, it's a process. Follow it, and you will be successful.

To learn about our training options or to engage a Certified Core Fit Hiring Coach, go to HireBetterPeopleFaster.com

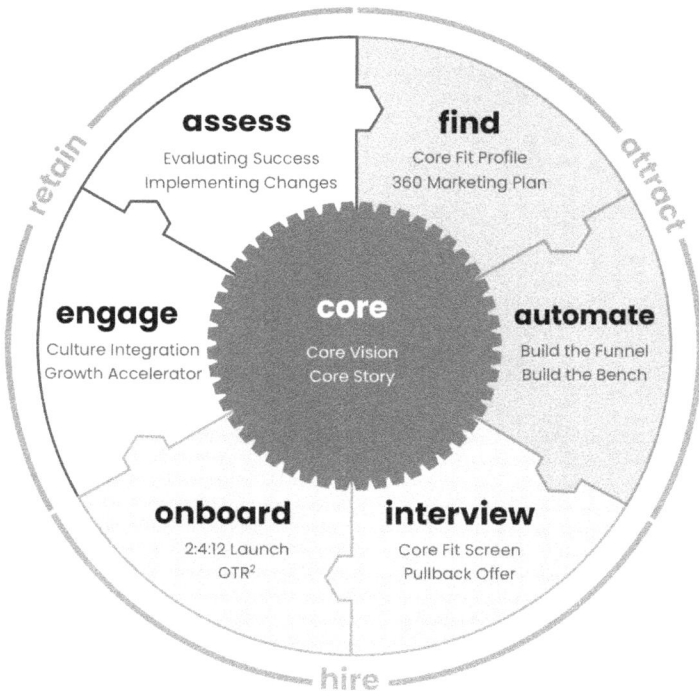

# Build Your Core:

Create Clarity to Lead

The struggles are real for many business owners. Struggling to manage cash, manage time, and manage the team and without structure and systems, the struggles continue. Structure frees creativity and creative business owners enjoy more freedom and more success.

Your company, your team, and your fellow leaders need a framework to operate in. Let us show you the proven steps we use to align your team around a vision, create the clarity and accountability to consistently drive the team forward, all while staying true to your core.

To learn about our training options, go to HireBetterPeopleFaster.com.

# Free Resources

Go to HireBetterPeopleFaster.com to access free resources, including:

- Interviews with business thought leaders about driving results in every area of your company
- Downloadable templates you can use to build your people process
- **A complete system for attracting, hiring, and retaining employees**
- **The 7 Questions Your Employees Need to Say Yes to!**
- ....and much more!

HireBetterPeopleFaster.com

# About the Authors

**Jeremy Macliver**

Jeremy Macliver hired his first person at age 19. For the first time, he was responsible for an employee's engagement, production, and paycheck. It was his first lesson on the importance of picking the right person. As a serial entrepreneur, Jeremy has led multiple companies through high-growth phases in construction, automotive, and service industries. Under Jeremy's leadership, companies have doubled in size year after year, created strong cultures that attracted top talent, increased profitability, won Best Places to Work, and created apprenticeship programs that support youths interested in getting into the trades.

Today, Jeremy shares his insights with leadership teams to reignite the passion on which their business was founded and guides them through the process of building a stable, long-lasting organization accountable to their vision.

Jeremy is a Certified EOS Implementer®, and lives with his wife and four children in Phoenix, Arizona.

Jeremy serves on the State of Arizona Advisory Board for Construction Education, chairs the State Welding Advisory Board, and oversees the SkillsUSA State Welding Competition.

Connect with Jeremy at thecorematters.com to learn more about how you can build a high performing team.

## Ryan Englin

Ryan worked in corporate America for over a decade mastering the art of how to build high-performing teams. He repeatedly built top-performing teams only to see them crushed by the corporate reshuffles. With all of the training and resources of corporate America at his fingertips, Ryan saw what worked and what did not. Ryan set out on a journey to build a system that could help ANY company attract, hire, and retain as much frontline top talent as they needed.

Today, Ryan works his proven system to help organizations systematically fill their open positions, increase employee communications, create clarity, reduce turnover, and build high-performing teams of front-line workers.

Ryan is the creator of the Core Fit Hiring System™ and is a Certified Core Fit Hiring Coach™ and lives in Phoenix, Arizona with his wife and two children.

Connect with Ryan at thecorematters.com to learn more about the Core Fit Hiring System or to engage a Certified Core Fit Hiring Coach so that you can attract, hire, and retain the people that fit you to the core!